D1311840

CATS SET VII

BIRMAN CATS

Kristin Petrie
ABDO Publishing Company

visit us at
www.abdopublishing.com

Published by ABDO Publishing Company, PO Box 398166, Minneapolis, MN 55439.
Copyright © 2014 by Abdo Consulting Group, Inc. International copyrights reserved
in all countries. No part of this book may be reproduced in any form without written
permission from the publisher. The Checkerboard Library™ is a trademark and logo of
ABDO Publishing Company.

Printed in the United States of America, North Mankato, Minnesota.
052013
092013

♻ PRINTED ON RECYCLED PAPER

Cover Photo: Photo by Helmi Flick
Interior Photos: Alamy pp. 7, 15, 19, 21; Getty Images pp. 16–17; Photos by Helmi Flick
    pp. 5, 9, 13; Thinkstock p. 11

Editors: Rochelle Baltzer, Tamara L. Britton
Art Direction: Neil Klinepier

Library of Congress Control Number: 2013932662

Cataloging-in-Publication Data

Petrie, Kristin.
 Birman cats / Kristin Petrie.
   p. cm. -- (Cats)
ISBN 978-1-61783-864-4
Includes bibliographical references and index.
1. Birman cat--Juvenile literature.   I. Title.
636.8--dc23

                                                              2013932662

CONTENTS

LIONS, TIGERS, AND CATS

Wild cats, **domestic** cats, big cats, and small cats! Cats come in all different sizes, colors, and personalities. However, they all have one thing in common. They are all members of the same family.

The family **Felidae** is large and varied. There are more than 37 species of cats in it. Lions, cougars, and bobcats are related to Persian, Siamese, and Maine coon cats!

Ancient Egyptians began to domesticate cats about 3,500 years ago. They wanted the cats to control the **rodent** population. Over time, cats became companion animals.

Humans continued to **breed** different types of cats to get certain looks and qualities. Today, there are more than 40 breeds of **domestic** cats. One of these is the beautiful Birman.

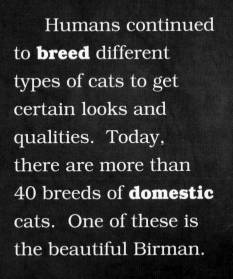

The Birman cat

BIRMAN CATS

Birman cats originated in Myanmar. This Asian country was previously known as Burma. There, Birman cats lived in religious temples. They were considered a sacred animal.

In 1919, one of these temples was attacked. Two men, Gordon Russell and August Pavie, helped save the temple's priests. The priests were grateful for their help.

Russell and Pavie later moved to France. To thank them, the priests sent the men a pair of Birman cats. The male did not survive the trip. But, the female cat arrived safely. And, she was **pregnant**! Her kittens established the Birman **breed** in the West.

France's cat registry recognized the breed in 1925. But by **World War II** the cats were almost extinct. Fans of the Birman saved the breed.

The first Birman cats arrived in the United States in 1959. In 1967, the **Cat Fanciers' Association (CFA)** recognized the Birman. By 2011, the Birman was the seventh most popular cat in the United States.

In Europe, the breed is known as the Sacred Cat of Burma.

QUALITIES

The Birman's positive qualities explain the **breed**'s popularity. Many owners describe their Birmans as social, playful, and entertaining. Other Birmans are reportedly mellow, observant, and loving. They will play for a while and then retreat to a quiet spot.

However, this spot out of the action will still be in the company of others! Birman cats love companionship. They make wonderful pets for people who spend much time at home. Those who are often away from home should consider a pet companion for their Birman.

Birman cats are calm and quiet. The Birman makes its needs known with a quiet meow. If necessary, it might give its owner a gentle nudge. For this reason, Birmans are often called "polite" cats.

Though polite, Birman cats can be bossy. If they want something, they will let you know!

COAT AND COLOR

The Birman's coat is medium to long. It is thicker around the cat's neck and slightly curly on its stomach. The coat's silky texture prevents it from **matting**.

The coat is a lighter color on the Birman's body. It is darker on its ears, face, legs, and tail. These areas are the cat's points.

The **CFA** recognizes four coat colors. Seal point Birmans have fawn to cream bodies and seal-brown points. Blue point Birmans have bluish-white to ivory bodies. Their points are blue.

Chocolate point Birmans have ivory bodies and chocolate-brown points. Lilac point cats have a white body. Their points are a light, pink-gray color.

A Birman's body is cooler at its points. This lower temperature makes the fur darker in these areas.

On a Birman's legs, its point color does not extend all the way to its toes. Bright white fur covers the paws. This creates the Birman's gloves. The white fur extends about halfway up the cat's back legs. There, the white fur is called laces.

SIZE

With its coat of thick, silky fur, the Birman looks like a very big cat. In reality, the **breed** is medium in size. However, the Birman's stocky body is solid and muscular. Males weigh up to 14 pounds (6 kg). Females can weigh up to 11 pounds (5 kg).

The Birman's furry neck holds a full, round head. Large, round eyes slant slightly upward toward rounded ears. The **muzzle** features a strong jaw and chin. The nose is dark and medium in size. Heavy, full cheeks sprout long whiskers.

The Birman's thick legs are medium in length. The rear legs are slightly longer than the front legs. Round paws and a bushy tail complete the Birman's **unique** appearance.

The male Birman is larger than the female.

CARE

Though the Birman's fur does not **mat**, it still needs proper grooming. A long-toothed metal or natural bristle brush is best for brushing. Birmans may also need an occasional bath. Use shampoo and conditioner made just for cats to maintain a healthy coat.

Your Birman's teeth will also need brushing. Bacteria can cause tooth decay and may cause illness. But do not use your own toothbrush! That's just gross. Toothbrushes and pastes made just for cats are much better for them.

You may need to trim your cat's claws. In the wild, cats trim their claws by scratching on trees and other objects. **Domestic** cats need to sharpen their claws too! So, be sure to provide a scratching post for your Birman. If you don't, it may scratch on the furniture!

Your cat will also have a natural instinct to bury its waste. It will need a **litter box**. Be sure to remove waste from the box every day.

Your cat will need a yearly visit to the veterinarian for an exam. The vet will also give your cat **vaccines**. He or she can **spay** or **neuter** your Birman, too.

There are different types of litter boxes and cat litters. You may have to try more than one to find a combination your cat is comfortable with.

FEEDING

Along with veterinarian visits, high-quality food is necessary for your Birman's health. Like humans, cats need a variety of **nutrients**. Protein helps them grow. Carbohydrates provide energy. Fats help many bodily functions.

Quality cat food comes in dry, semimoist, and canned versions. Many owners prefer dry cat food because it does not spoil. In addition, it cleans the teeth while the cat chews.

Many cats prefer canned food. Most owners providing this food feed their cats twice a day. This way, no food is left out to spoil. No matter which food your cat prefers, make sure you provide fresh water every day.

Amino acids are the building blocks of body tissues. One of these is taurine, which a cat's body cannot produce. Cats must eat a meat-based diet to get this essential nutrient.

KITTENS

Birman cats are ready to reproduce at five to six months of age. After mating, a mother Birman is **pregnant** for about 65 days. She usually gives birth to four kittens in her **litter**.

The newborn kittens are blind and deaf. When they are two weeks old, they begin to see and hear. After about three weeks, the kittens begin to play and explore their surroundings. And, their teeth start to come in.

The kittens will drink milk from their mother for about five weeks. At six weeks of age, they begin to eat solid foods. However, they may start to sneak food from their mother's bowl before then!

Birman kittens should be handled every day. Daily contact will create calm, friendly pets. When the kittens are 12 to 16 weeks old, they are ready to be adopted.

Birman kittens are born white. When they are about one week old, their points begin to show color. The points continue to darken throughout their first year of life.

BUYING A KITTEN

Are you ready to adopt a Birman? If so, you will need to make a few decisions. For example, do you want a kitten or a cat? Kittens are fun and adorable. But, they also come with lots of surprises, costs, and work!

Kittens need **vaccinations** and **spaying** or **neutering**. Before you bring your kitten home, you will need to buy a few supplies. A **litter box**, a scratching post, food, and grooming tools are good to start.

Also, kittens need training. Plan to be home often during training time. Otherwise, your home may be their playground and their litter box!

Many adult cats, on the other hand, may already be trained and spayed or neutered. They have already had their vaccines. Their personalities

Birman cats are great companion cats!

and coats are developed. You will know what you are
getting!

Whether you choose a kitten or a cat, look for a
reputable **breeder**. Good breeders tell buyers about a
kitten's health history and needs. A healthy and happy
Birman will be a loving companion for about 15 years.

GLOSSARY

breed - a group of animals sharing the same ancestors and appearance. A breeder is a person who raises animals. Raising animals is often called breeding them.

Cat Fanciers' Association (CFA) - a group that sets the standards for judging all breeds of cats.

domestic - tame, especially relating to animals.

Felidae (FEHL-uh-dee) - the scientific Latin name for the cat family. Members of this family are called felids. They include lions, tigers, leopards, jaguars, cougars, wildcats, lynx, cheetahs, and domestic cats.

litter - all of the kittens born at one time to a mother cat.

litter box - a box filled with cat litter, which is similar to sand. Cats use litter boxes to bury their waste.

mat - to form into a tangled mass.

muzzle - an animal's nose and jaws.

neuter (NOO-tuhr) - to remove a male animal's reproductive glands.

nutrient - a substance found in food and used in the body. It promotes growth, maintenance, and repair.

pregnant - having one or more babies growing within the body.

rodent - any of several related animals that have large front teeth for gnawing. Common rodents include mice, squirrels, and beavers.

spay - to remove a female animal's reproductive organs.

unique - being the only one of its kind.

vaccine (vak-SEEN) - a shot given to prevent illness or disease.

World War II - from 1939 to 1945, fought in Europe, Asia, and Africa.

WEB SITES

To learn more about Birman cats, visit ABDO Publishing Company online. Web sites about Birman cats are featured on our Book Links page. These links are routinely monitored and updated to provide the most current information available.

www.abdopublishing.com

INDEX